St. Aloysius Parish
OF LEONARDTOWN, MARYLAND

THE EXACT ORIGINS OF THE CATHOLIC COMMUNITY which developed into St. Aloysius parish remain obscure. In 1708 it was decided that the County court house for St. Mary's would be moved from Newtown to a new, more central location, at the head of Bretton Bay. The community that grew up around the court house was known as "Seymour Town" until 1728 when the name was changed to Leonardtown. It is assumed by local historians that since Catholics were numerous in St. Mary's County, and in fact constituted a majority of its population by 1734, there must have been Catholics in Leonardtown. It is further assumed that these Leonardtown area Catholics must have gathered for Mass which would have been offered by one of the Jesuit priests who lived at Newtown. Thus, for some time now, the establishment of the parish has been dated to around 1710.

The earliest written documentation we have for St. Aloysius parish comes from the diary of Father James Walton, S.J. who described the raising of funds to erect the first church in 1766 while he was pastor at Newtown (St. Francis Xavier). This church was located approximately two miles north of the site of the current church and served the community until 1846. Although the church Fr. Walton had erected is long gone, the cemetery that surrounded it is still open today.

The second documented church of St. Aloysius was erected in 1846 under the direction of Fr. Joseph Enders, S.J. , who was the Superior at Newtown at that time. Designed by a parishioner, Vincent Camalier, this brick structure, which stood on the south side of the current rectory, was approximately 95 feet in length and 44 feet wide and served the community until 1959. In 1866, the Jesuit residence at Newtown was moved to Leonardtown and St. Aloysius became the center of Catholic life in the upper part of St. Mary's County. In 1885 the Sisters of Charity of Nazareth, Kentucky opened St. Mary's Academy here at the behest of the current pastor, Fr. Charles Jenkins, S.J., The Xaverian Brothers opened Leonard Hall in the parish as a school for boys in 1909. To these educational institutions located in the parish were added Father Andrew White elementary school in 1954 and Ryken High School in 1956. St. Mary's Academy and Ryken High School merged in 1981.

Since the departure of the Jesuit priests in 1964 the parish has been staffed by diocesan priests and currently (June 2001) serves 850 families. Ever grateful for the gift of our Catholic heritage and trusting in the intercession of our patron saint, the people and priests of St. Aloysius parish pledge ourselves to furthering the mission of Christ in our community.

The Truth in Charity:
A HISTORY OF
The Archdiocese of Washington

BY

REV. RORY T. CONLEY, PH.D.

Dear Bob,

I hope this is up to the standards you taught me.

Rory

September 2001

Cross on St. Clement's Island, where Mass was first held in 1634

Text by:
The Reverend Rory T. CONLEY, Ph. D.

Photos by:
Mike HOYT

Layout:
Juliette ROUSSEL

Publishing Director:
Christian RIEHL

Director of Publications:
Dr. Claude-Bernard COSTECALDE

Published by:
Éditions du Signe
1, rue Alfred Kastler
67038 Strasbourg, Cedex 2 – France
Tel: (33) 3 88 78 91 91 / Fax (33) 3 88 78 91 99

Table of Contents

The view from Loyola Retreat House, operated by the Society of Jesus at Faulkner in Charles County.

Theodore Cardinal McCarrick, Archbishop of Washington

Preface

A S WE BEGIN *the third Christian millennium, celebrating Christ's abiding presence with us in the Blessed Sacrament, it is fitting that we remember how the Lord was also present to our Catholic forbears who brought the faith to this land. This brief history of our Archdiocese can only present in summary form an account of all that has happened here since a small group of pilgrims offered the Mass for the first time on St. Clement's Island in 1634. However, it is hoped that this account will inspire in its readers a sense of gratitude for all the men and women, clergy, religious and laity, who labored so hard so that the Catholic faith may be handed on to us. We have so much to be grateful for.*

Should readers wish to learn more about our local Catholic history they are encouraged to consult the following works: The Jesuit Missions of St. Mary's County (1976) by Edwin W. Beitzell; The Premier See: A History of the Archdiocese of Baltimore, 1789-1989 (1989) by Thomas W. Spalding; A Parish for the Federal City: St. Patrick's in Washington, 1794-1994 (1994) by Morris J. MacGregor; At Peace With All Their Neighbors: Catholics and Catholicism in the National Capital, 1787-1860 (1994) by William W. Warner and The Emergence of A Black Catholic Community: St. Augustine's in Washington (1999) by Morris J. MacGregor. Most of our parishes have their own written histories which describe in greater detail the accomplishments of our local Catholic communities.

The author wishes to thank Susan Gibbs, Director of the Archdiocesan Office of Communications; Deacon Bernard Bernier, Archivist of the Archdiocese; Mark Adkinson and Michael Hoyt for their invaluable assistance in providing photographs and illustrations to accompany the text. Ms. Gibbs and Deacon Bernier are also to be thanked for their editorial suggestions. My gratitude is also owed to Rev. Msgr. Robert O. McMain, Historian of the Archdiocese, Morris J. MacGregor, Brother Randal Reide, C.F.X. and Rev David H. Werning for their helpful advice in preparing the text.

Rev. Rory T. Conley, Ph. D.
April 2001

PART 1

The Colonial Period, 1634-1773

The Founding: "Worthy of Angels "

"On the day of the Annunciation of the Most Holy Virgin Mary, in the year 1634, we celebrated on this island the first Mass which had been offered up in this part of the world. After we had completed the Sacrifice, we took upon our shoulders a great cross which we had shaped out of a tree and advancing in order to the appointed place, with the assistance of the Governor and his associates and the other Catholics, we erected a trophy to Christ the Savior, humbly reciting on our knees the Litanies of the Holy Cross with great emotion."

WITH THESE WORDS Father Andrew White, S.J. (1579-1656) memorialized the founding of Maryland and the first celebration of the Mass in the English-speaking colonies. It would be 306 years later to the day that the first Archbishop of Washington, Michael J. Curley, was installed at the Cathedral of St. Matthew. But it was here, on March 25, 1634, on St. Clement's Island in St. Mary's County, that the history of the Archdiocese of Washington began. The journey to that first Mass on territory, which is now part of the Archdiocese of Washington, was a bit of a pilgrimage for those involved.

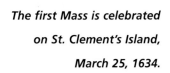

The first Mass is celebrated on St. Clement's Island, March 25, 1634.

*Fr. Andrew White, S.J. (1579-1656)
was the "Apostle of Maryland."*

The roughly 150 men, women and children who raised the cross at St. Clement's Island on that day had made their journey for different reasons. For some, most certainly Father Andrew White and his fellow Jesuits, Father John Waltham and Brother Thomas Gervase, the journey to Lord Baltimore's new colony of Maryland had been undertaken precisely so that the cross of Christ could be raised and the Gospel proclaimed there not only for the benefit of their fellow colonists, but also for the sake of the native peoples they had come to evangelize. While little is known about Waltham or Gervase other than that they both died within a few years of their arrival in Maryland, Father Andrew White played an indispensable role in the founding of the colony.

The oldest member of the expedition, White had studied at the English colleges at Valladolid and Douai, and was ordained a secular priest in 1605. Father White's initial assignment on the English mission was cut short after a few months when he was arrested and banished from England for life in the aftermath of the failed Gunpowder Plot. In 1606 he entered the Society of Jesus and in the intervening years had served as a Professor of Sacred Scripture at various colleges on the Continent. Chosen by his superiors to be the leader of the Jesuits on the Maryland mission, Father White was an enthusiastic supporter of the endeavor. After his selection, White corresponded with the first Lord Baltimore, George Calvert (+1632), regarding plans for Maryland and in 1633 he wrote a promotional tract about the venture at the request of the second Lord Baltimore and founder of the colony, Cecilius Calvert (1606-1675). Father Andrew White also left to history his invaluable *Relation of the Successful beginnings of Lord Baltimore's Plantation in Mary-land*, which recounts the first days of the colony. In keeping with the missionary ardor that characterized the Society of Jesus, Father White and his companions possessed an apostolic zeal to bring the Gospel of Christ to the native peoples while nurturing the faith of the Catholic colonists. Manifesting his own belief as to the supernatural benefits the Maryland settlement would bring to the native peoples, and invoking a play on words first invoked at the time of the evangelization of England, Father White promoted the venture as being "worthy of Christians, worthy of angels, worthy of Englishmen."

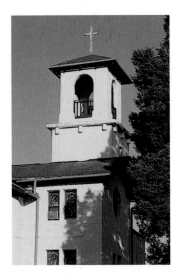

Our Lady's Church at Medley's Neck, Medley's Neck

thoroughly alienated from the Calvert family, which had founded the colony as a haven for Catholics, and the colonial assembly, in which they no longer had much influence. Another

Sacred Heart, Bushwood

connection to those first hopeful days of Maryland's founding was severed in 1773 when Europe's political situation led to the official suppression of the Society of Jesus by Pope Clement XIV. Fortunately, the approximately 20 now ex-Jesuit priests in Maryland soon reorganized themselves as the Corporation of Roman Catholic Clergy and elected to stay on the Maryland mission. This is despite the lack of an official mandate or any way of replenishing their ranks. It was under these trying circumstances that Maryland's Catholics entered America's, and their own, fight for liberty.

St. Joseph, Morganza

St. Ignatius in Oxon Hill was established as a mission of Upper Marlboro in 1849.

Most Holy Rosary in Rosaryville was established by the Dominicans in 1859 as a successor to Boone's Chapel.

delayed the opening of St. Mary's until 1829, when the Jesuits reluctantly conceded. The Jesuits continued to serve St. Mary's from their residence at White Marsh for the next 27 years. Responding to new pastoral needs in the Oxon Hill area of the county, the Jesuits erected another mission church there, St. Ignatius, in 1849. In 1856 the care of the Marlboro church mission was given to the Dominicans. The Dominicans' tenure at St. Mary's lasted only 13 years but within that time, under the leadership of Father Nicholas Young and through the beneficence of the Mitchell family, they succeeded in erecting a new church in 1859 for the congregation of Boone's Chapel.

Reflecting the traditional devotion to the rosary held by the sons of St. Dominic, the new church, a mission of St. Mary's in Marlboro, was named Most Holy Rosary. When the Dominicans ended their work in Prince George's County in 1869, they were succeeded by the Carmelite Fathers, who served the congregations at Upper Marlboro, Rosaryville, Oxon Hill and Piscataway until 1875.

For most of the period between the Revolution and the Civil War Catholics at the southern end of Prince George's County were served by priests traveling from Charles County. Sometimes the priests who came to offer the Mass, baptize the children, marry the engaged and bury the dead came from the Jesuit residence of St. Thomas Manor at Chapel Point. Others were Sulpicians, Dominicans or diocesan priests who lived either at Lower Zekiah, which was the name for St. Mary's, Bryantown or at Upper Zekiah, now St. Peter's in Waldorf. When priests didn't come north from Charles County, they usually came from St. Mary's at Upper Marlboro.

The first church to be erected in the area was St. Mary's in Piscataway, built in 1838. Prior to the erection of St. Mary's, the Catholic community in the southeastern corner of the county near the Potomac were served by the family chapels owned by the Digges of Warburton (now part of Fort Washington

National Park), William Digges of Frankland (near Tinker Creek) and Mattowoman Chapel, originally owned by the Middleton family, located on the boundary with Charles County. Of course, all of these chapels were preceded by the family chapel of the Piscataway chief, Chitomachen, who was baptized at Kattamaquindi (now part of Piscataway National Park) by Father Andrew White in 1640.

The sixth parish to be established in Prince George's County prior to the Civil War was St. Mary of the Mills in Laurel. Located on the western bank of the Patuxent River, Laurel became the site of an important gristmill in 1811. By the 1820's the town boasted a textile mill and iron foundry. In the early 1830's, a young doctor, Theodore Jenkins, opened his home for the celebration of Masses offered by Jesuits from Georgetown where Jenkins had been educated. The coming of the Washington to Baltimore route of the B & O Railroad in 1835 facilitated the Jesuits' ministry in the town. Through the further generosity of Dr. Jenkins, the first Mass at the new stone church of St. Mary of the Mills was offered by Father James Ryder, president of Georgetown College, on January 22, 1843. The Jesuits continued to serve at St. Mary's in Laurel until 1866 when the parish was turned over to the care of the diocesan clergy.

St. Mary of the Mills in Laurel.

Dr. Theodore Jennings, after first opening his home to Catholics in the Laurel area for the celebration of the Eucharist in the 1830's, financed the erection of St. Mary's Chapel where the first Mass was offered on January 22, 1843.

"Piety Everywhere Revived": Charles County

WHILE THE CATHOLICS OF THE DISTRICT, Montgomery and Prince George's Counties were busy laying the foundations of new churches and parishes in the decades between the Revolution and the Civil War, the challenge for the Catholics of Southern Maryland in this period was to improve what they already possessed. In Charles County there were already eight well-established Catholic congregations by 1800. In 1818 these congregations were each visited by Archbishop Maréchal who recorded his impressions of the communities in his diary. The oldest of these, of course, was St. Ignatius at Chapel Point, which dates back to 1641. At the time of Maréchal's visit, the church had some 800 congregants. The residence there, named St. Thomas Manor, was the home base for the Jesuits. The next two oldest congregations in Charles County, St. Mary's at Newport and St. Mary's at Bryantown, can both trace their origins to family chapels that existed in their respective areas in the late 1600's.

St. Mary's at Newport has the unique distinction among all parishes in the Archdiocese of being founded by the Franciscans in the person of Father Basil Hobart, O.F.M., who arrived there in 1674. At the time of Father Hobart's arrival, Newport, near the Wicomico River, was one of the two most important port towns in Charles County.

Father Hobart apparently was responsible for the construction of the first church there in 1677. He continued to serve the Catholics of Newport until his death during an epidemic in 1698. Following the death of Father Hobart, the congregation at Newport was taken into the care of the Jesuits. They continued to serve there until 1881, at which point the parish began to be staffed by diocesan priests. When Archbishop Maréchal visited the Catholics at Newport in 1818 he noted their well-decorated church and later praised the "generous zeal" of the 800 Catholics in the parish.

The roots of the Catholic community at Bryantown extend back at least to the 1690's when the Jesuit fathers attended a chapel on the estate of Major William Boarman. Throughout the eighteenth century, Catholics worshipped in a log chapel in the area. In 1793 this structure was replaced by a simple frame church which was dedicated by then-Bishop John Carroll on August 15 of that year. A few months before the erection of the church, Lower Zekiah (Bryantown) had received its first resident pastor, a young French Sulpician, Father Jean Baptiste Maria David. Father David spent some 12 years serving the Catholics in both northern

St. Mary in Bryantown traces its origins to the 1690's. It was preceded by a log chapel which was dedicated by Bishop John Carroll in 1793.

Charles and southern Prince George's Counties ministering to the communities at Lower Zekiah, Upper Zekiah (St. Peter's, Waldorf) and at Mattawoman chapel. These congregations had never before received such zealous care and David's first biographer noted that "piety everywhere revived..." Called away from Charles County by Bishop Carroll in 1804, Father David went on to hold posts at Georgetown, St. Mary's Seminary in Baltimore, and Mount St. Mary's in

St. Mary in Bryantown

Emmitsburg. He was instrumental in founding the Sisters of Charity of Nazareth, Kentucky and was eventually named the Bishop of Bardstown.

Although he did not stay long, the next pastor of both St. Mary's and St. Peter's, Edward Dominic Fenwick, O.P., was to become an important figure in American Catholic history as founder of the American branch of the Dominican order and the first bishop of Cincinnati. At the time of Archbishop Maréchal's 1818 visit, Lower Zekiah (Bryantown) and Upper Zekiah (Waldorf) were being tended by another Dominican, Father Robert Angier. After Father Angier returned to his native England in 1825, St. Mary's at Lower Zekiah and the parish at Upper Zekiah were placed under the care of diocesan clergy, although there were a

couple of intervals when the Jesuits from Chapel Point were called upon to fill a vacancy. In 1846 a new church was built under the direction of Father Patrick Courtney and by 1859 the parish was sponsoring an "academy for young ladies." In 1852 the Catholic community at Upper Zekiah, which was also called "Reeves" and "Beantown" and is now known as Waldorf, was officially separated from Bryantown and placed under the care of Father John Donelan, who was also pastor of St. Mary's at Piscatway, where he lived. His successor, Father Peter Lenaghan, who served the community there from 1855 until 1874, erected a new church dedicated to St. Peter around 1860.

Some 15 miles west of Upper and Lower Zekiah, St. Joseph's was opened at Pomfret in 1763 by Father George Hunter, S.J. who, at the time, was superior of the Jesuit mission at Chapel Point. It appears that in establishing this church Father Hunter was simply assuming responsibility for a chapel that already existed there on the property of George Clements, who had sold him the land. By 1818, St. Joseph's, Pomfret had a congregation of some 500 people. Another Charles County congregation which formed originally at a family chapel was St. Charles at Glymont, near Indian Head. This community

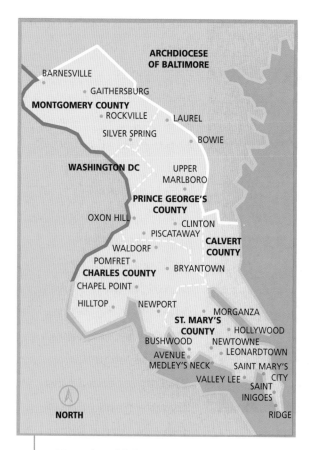

ARCHDIOCESE
OF BALTIMORE

BARNESVILLE
GAITHERSBURG
MONTGOMERY COUNTY
ROCKVILLE   LAUREL
SILVER SPRING
BOWIE
WASHINGTON DC   UPPER
MARLBORO
PRINCE GEORGE'S
COUNTY
OXON HILL   CLINTON
PISCATAWAY
WALDORF   CALVERT
COUNTY
POMFRET   BRYANTOWN
CHARLES COUNTY
CHAPEL POINT
HILLTOP   NEWPORT
MORGANZA
ST. MARY'S
COUNTY   HOLLYWOOD
BUSHWOOD   NEWTOWNE
AVENUE   LEONARDTOWN
MEDLEY'S NECK
VALLEY LEE   SAINT MARY'S
CITY
SAINT
INIGOES
NORTH   RIDGE

Map of parish locations in 1860.

gathered for Mass as early as 1750 at the home of the Pye family at what was then called "Cornwallis Neck." In 1800 the Pye family deeded an one and one-half acres to Father Jean Montdesir, a young Frenchman who had been ordained for the Archdiocese of Baltimore only the year before. Father Montdesir, who had been given charge of the congregation at Pomfret as well, quickly built a church at Cornwallis Neck and placed it under the patronage of St. Charles Borromeo. After Father Montdesir's departure in 1804, the pastoral care of St. Charles passed to the Jesuits. When Archbishop Maréchal came there in 1818 the congregation numbered some 400 persons.

In addition to the six congregations already mentioned, Archbishop Maréchal visited two other, smaller Catholic communities in Charles County during his 1818 trip. The first of these was the Catholic community at Nanjemoy where Maréchal counted some 100 souls and which, with other Catholics in western Charles County, would form the parish of St. Ignatius, Hilltop in the 1850's. The other congregation was the one at "Cub Neck," near present day Cobb Island, which in 1818 had 250 members.

During his pastoral visit to Charles County, Archbishop Maréchal made a special point of visiting the Carmelite monastery located some two miles north of Port Tobacco, where he presided at the election of the community's prioress. The opening of Mount Carmel near Port Tobacco on October 15, 1790 made it the first community of women religious to be established in the United States. It was very much a Charles County affair. The first three sisters, the superior, Mother Bernadina Theresa Xavier (Ann Matthews), and her two nieces, Sister Mary Aloysia (Ann Theresa Matthews) and Sister Mary Eleanor (Susanna Matthews), were natives of Charles County. The community's principal benefactor and spiritual director, Father Charles Neale, was also their kinsman. At the time of Archbishop

Commemorative coin marking the bicentennial of the Carmel at Port Tobacco. When founded in 1790, the Carmel was the first community of women religious to be established in the United States.

Maréchal's visit in 1818 the community was flourishing. According to his account, the Carmel was "extremely neat & decent." However, by 1831, the Carmelites found it increasingly difficult to survive on the income from their farm. So they sold their property in Charles County and moved to Baltimore, where the fourth Archbishop of Baltimore, James Whitfield, prevailed upon them to open a school for girls. A century and a half later, Carmelite nuns returned to Charles County and the site of the first monastery in the United States.

A Carmelite nun at Port Tobacco today. Established by Charles County natives in 1790, the Carmelites were forced by hard times to move to Baltimore in 1831. Nearly a century and a half later, Carmelite nuns returned to Port Tobacco.

"Living Love our Holy Religion" St. Mary's County

AS THE HOME OF THE EARLIEST SETTLEMENTS in Maryland and with a comparatively large Catholic population, St. Mary's County had seven well-established Catholic communities which regularly gathered for the celebration of the Mass by the time of the American Revolution. Another church was added around 1795 when the great builder, Father Joseph Walton, S.J., erected the first church of St. Nicholas at Mattapany. This church served area Catholics who previously attended Mass in various family chapels. In the middle decades of the nineteenth century two more parishes were established in the county. The first of these was

St. Michael's in Ridge, established around 1830 to serve Catholics who lived south of St. Inigoes. To the north of St. Inigoes, St. George's parish was established in 1851 on property donated by John Shadrick, a non-Catholic. Thus, by the time of the Civil War, there were ten Catholic churches in St. Mary's County. All but St. Ignatius at St. Inigoes and St. Nicholas at the Patuxent Naval Air Station are now active parishes in the Archdiocese of Washington.

Catholics in St. Mary's County remained under the care of priests associated with the Society of Jesus throughout the nineteenth century. Thirty-two years after the suppression

of the Jesuits, the Society of Jesus was able to reestablish itself in 1805. Operating from their farms at Newtown and St. Inigoes, the "new" Jesuits continued the tradition of their forerunners by riding a circuit around to the churches of the county. At times a few secular priests, such as Father James Vanhuffel, who served at St. Aloysius from 1792-1814, and Father James Griffin at St. Joseph's in Morganza from 1800-1814, also served in St. Mary's County. In 1813 a small band of French Trappists arrived to establish a monastery near St. Nicholas. Despite difficult circumstances they survived the winter only to be driven out by the heat, mosquitoes and fevers of summer.

While the summer heat plagued many a newcomer, Catholic visitors then and now have been pleasantly warmed by the fire of faith which has continued to burn among the Catholics of St. Mary's County. As part of the "Jubilee Mission" of 1830, during which the Jesuits traveled to all of the county's churches over a 33-day period preaching a mission, a

French Jesuit, Father Stephen Dubuisson, observed the religious fervor that still existed in the birthplace of Maryland Catholicism: "The persevering attendance of the people at the exercises was wonderful...Words cannot express the consolation that filled my soul when I was brought face to face with the living love for our holy religion."

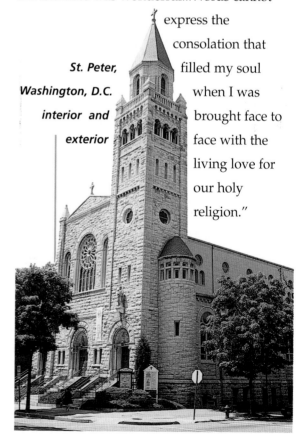

St. Peter, Washington, D.C. interior and exterior

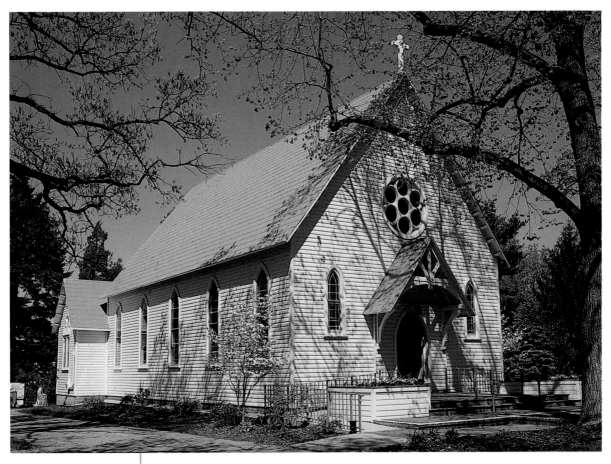

St. Rose of Lima, Gaithersburg (old and new churches)

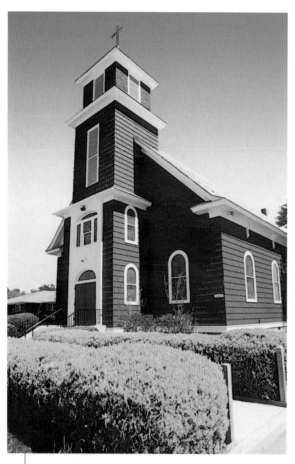

St. Michael, Ridge

St. Ignatius, Hilltop

St. George, Valley Lee

St. Peter, Olney

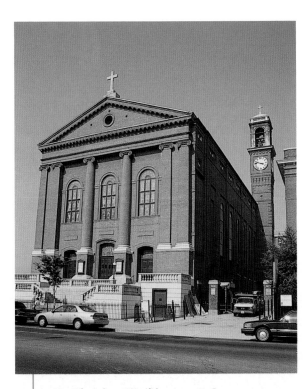

St. Aloysius, Washington, D.C.

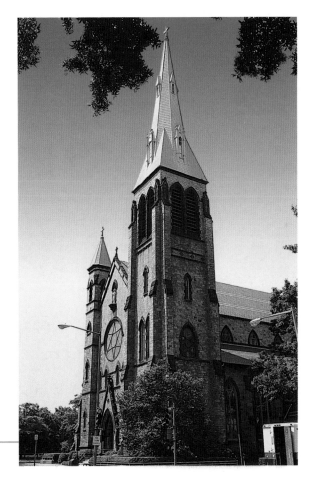

St. Dominic, Washington, D.C.

St. Ann, Washington D.C.

St. Stephen Martyr, Washington, D.C.

St. John the Evangelist, Clinton

Following a hiatus of five years, reflecting no doubt the downturn of the national economy, a veritable storm of church building took place in Washington between 1899 and 1905. To keep up with the rapid expansion of the city six new parishes were begun in seven years: three in Northwest, Nativity (1899), Sacred Heart (1899) and St. Martin (1901); two in Northeast, Holy Comforter (1904) and

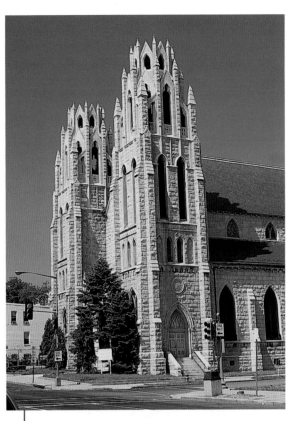

St. Augustine, Washington, D.C. now is located in the original St. Paul parish church on V Street, N.W.

St. Teresa of Avila, Washington, D.C

Holy Name, Washington, D.C.

St. Anthony of Padua, Washington, D.C.

St. James (1905); and one in Southwest, the previously mentioned parish of St. Vincent de Paul (1903). A similar building boom occurred between 1909 and 1916 with the Northwest quadrant of the city requiring three more parishes, Our Lady of Victory (1909), Blessed Sacrament (1910), and St. Thomas (1913). In 1913 Holy Rosary parish opened to minister to the needs of the Italian community which had developed around Union Station. Incarnation parish in Northeast was begun for blacks in 1914 as a mission of St. Margaret's parish. Then, in 1916, Southeast Washington received its second parish when the Church of the Assumption

was opened. Three years later St. Gabriel's parish opened at Grant Circle, N.W.

Holy Rosary parish was established in 1913 to serve the Italian speaking community in Washington.

Degrees, Dignitaries and the Dome

THE ESTABLISHMENT OF 16 NEW PARISHES, most of which also had elementary schools, during the 50 years between the end of the Civil War and the First World War was necessitated by the growth of the city's population from some 170,000 persons to approximately 400,000. Unlike other larger cities, including Baltimore, the growth of Washington in these decades was not due to the advances of modern industrial production

and the concurrent migration of an ethnic, immigrant work force. Rather, in a process that continues into the present, Washington grew in size as the federal government's role in national life increased and as the United States assumed greater stature in world affairs. The maturing of Washington as the national capital of an emerging world power also led to the District being the site of several Catholic institutions with international importance.

The first of these was The Catholic University of America, officially approved by the bishops of the United States in 1884. Guided initially by the inspiration of Bishop John Lancaster Spalding of Peoria, Illinois, and administered by Bishop John J. Keane, its first rector, the University was chartered by Pope Leo XIII in March 1889. It officially opened in November of that same year. The Catholic University was conceived as a post-graduate level institution which would further the progress of Catholics in American national life. It would also be a sign that the Church in the United States was coming of age. Thus, it was with great pride and a sense of accomplishment that Catholics from around the nation, including much of the hierarchy, gathered with thousands of local Catholics under the leadership of Cardinal James Gibbons of Baltimore to welcome President Grover Cleveland to the laying of the cornerstone for the new university on May 24, 1888.

It should be noted that the presence of President Cleveland at this ceremony, and then again 18 months later for the official opening, was a tribute both to Catholic citizens in general and to Cardinal Gibbons in particular. Born in Baltimore in 1834 of Irish immigrant parents, James Gibbons became the ninth Archbishop of Baltimore

The dedication ceremony for The Catholic University of America in 1888 drew President Grover Cleveland. James Cardinal Gibbons, Archbishop of Baltimore, presided.

in 1877 and was elected to the College of Cardinals in 1886. He led the Archdiocese for 46 years until his death in 1921. Personable and outgoing, Cardinal Gibbons was the genial primate of the Catholic Church in

McMahon Building at The Catholic University of America

James Cardinal Gibbons (1834-1921).
Following his appointment as Archbishop
of Baltimore in 1877, Gibbons served for
44 years as the de facto primate of the
Catholic Church in America. Recognized
throughout the country, his friendliness
and gentle demeanor did much to alleviate
prejudice against Catholics.

America throughout his tenure and did much to gain acceptance for Catholics in American society at a time when there was intense hostility toward Catholic immigrants. A friend of presidents and advocate for workers, no bishop who has served in Washington has played a larger role on the national stage. For many Americans of his

day, including non-Catholics, Cardinal Gibbons was one of the capital's leading figures.

The importance of Washington as the capital of the United States soon brought other Catholic institutions of national importance to the District. The Apostolic Delegation to the United States was established in 1893 to officially represent the pope to both the federal government and the American hierarchy. Later, when the United States extended diplomatic recognition to the Holy See in the 1980's, the papal delegation in Washington was elevated to the status of a nunciature. During the First World War the American bishops established an organization in Washington whose purpose was to promote and unify all Catholic activities in the United States related to the war effort. With the cessation of hostilities this organization, renamed the National Conference of Catholic Bishops, has continued into the present its efforts to coordinate various forms of Catholic action in the United States. Another addition to Catholic Washington around the turn of the twentieth century was Trinity College. At that time neither Georgetown University nor Catholic University accepted women. So the Sisters of Notre Dame de Namur established Trinity College in 1897, welcoming its first students in 1900. Since that time Trinity has remained one of the leading Catholic liberal arts colleges for women in America.

In 1913 efforts were initiated to erect a shrine in honor of the patroness of the United States, the Blessed Virgin Mary, under her title of the Immaculate Conception.

The Apostolic Nunciature was established in 1893. Its present building was erected in the 1930's, largely through the efforts of Archbishop Michael J. Curley.

The National Conference of Catholic Bishops began meeting during World War I. The current building near The Catholic University was built in the 1980's.

Sr. Julia McGroarty, founder of Trinity College. Trinity was established to provide Catholic women with the opportunity for a college education.

The construction of this monument of faith, the Basilica of the National Shrine of the Immaculate Conception, began in November 1920 when Cardinal Gibbons laid the cornerstone four months before his death. The Crypt Church was completed in 1926, but the onset of the Depression and then the Second World War brought construction to a halt. Work on the Great Upper Church resumed in 1954 and on November 20, 1959 this shrine to Mary, the largest Catholic church in the Western Hemisphere, was dedicated at a Mass celebrated by Francis Cardinal Spellman of New York with most of the American hierarchy and thousands of other Catholics assisting. Forty years later, in November 1999, the interior decoration was essentially completed with the dedication of a large sculpture over the main entrance commemorating the "Universal Call to Holiness" of each of the baptized. The

Francisan Monastery of the Holy Land, Washington, D.C. was established in 1899. The Shrine includes replicas of the significant Holy Land sites as well as beautiful gardens.

Trinity College in Washington, established by the Sisters of Notre Dame de Namur, is one of the oldest Catholic liberal arts colleges for women in the country.

Basilica of the National Shrine of the Immaculate Conception with its distinctive dome has become a landmark of Catholicism in Washington and in America.

In addition to establishing important buildings and educational institutions, Washington-area Catholics of the late nineteenth and early twentieth centuries, like Catholics elsewhere, in fact, like Americans everywhere, were terrific "joiners." They joined all types of organizations: pious societies such as the Holy Name and Sodality, benevolent associations and fraternal groups like the Knights of Columbus and the Knights of St. John and even, for the more intellectually inclined, literary societies such as the Carroll Institute. These organizations, which often corresponded to similar groups supported by non-Catholics, played an important role in building cohesiveness

The Basilica of the National Shrine of the Immaculate Conception was initiated in 1913 and dedicated in 1959. One of the largest churches in the world, its beautiful dome has become a beloved landmark in the nation's capital.

Holy Name Society Rally at Washington Monument 1924 with President Coolidge. Although anti-Catholicism was still rampant in the 1920's, and was particularly virulent as a result of Gov. Al Smith's nomination for president in 1928, Catholics represented a major force in American life.

Mary Virginia Merrick (1866-1955), founder of the Christ Child Society. Although paralyzed by an accident in her teens, Merrick was an energetic advocate for poor children. Merrick established the Christ Child Society in Washington in 1887 to provide direct service to poor children based on Catholic principles. By 1916 the Christ Child Society was organized nationally with chapters in numerous cities. The Society continues to serve at-risk children with more than 8,000 members in over 40 chapters in 18 states.

within the Catholic community and preserving their identity within America's pluralistic society.

These various voluntary associations remained a vital part of American Catholic life into the 1960's.

The Knights of St. John (left) and the Knights of Columbus (right) have become an integral part of Archdiocesan life. These fraternal organizations promote spirituality and service to the Church. Members often serve as color guards for the archbishop and auxiliary bishops.

As It Was In The Beginning: The Five Counties

WHILE THE DISTRICT'S POPULATION more than tripled in the decades between 1870 and 1920, the surrounding counties saw only marginal increases. In fact, the three southernmost counties, St. Mary's, Charles and Calvert, actually had fewer residents at the end of the nineteenth century than they did at its beginning. Under these circumstances, not surprisingly, the Church grew very slowly in what was still an overwhelmingly agricultural environment.

During the 50-year period under discussion, Montgomery County added four new Catholic parishes to the five which predated the Civil War. The first of these new congregations, St. Gabriel's at Great Falls, was established in 1890 as a mission of St. Ann's in the District to address the needs of Catholics in the Potomac area. However, when the C & O Canal ceased to function as a commercial trading route in the 1920's and when the nearby gold mines which had attracted

Slow growth in St. Mary's County, which had ten Catholic churches at the time of the Civil War to serve a total population of 15,213 persons, meant of only two more parishes were established in the nineteenth century, Immaculate Conception in Mechanicsville (1876) and Holy Face at Great Mills (1879), plus one mission, St. Francis Xavier on St. George's Island (1893). In 1900 the County's population reached 17,182 but then fell by 1,000 over the next 20 years. Still with more priests available, four more churches were added during this period. The multiplication of churches not only reduced traveling distances in the days before the automobile, it also facilitated evangelization. The first of these new churches, St. Peter Claver in Ridge, was established at the request of blacks in the region who rebelled against the segregationist policies then in practice at St. Michael's. The chapel of St. Mary's at California was established in 1912 a few miles south of Hollywood and was tended to by the priests serving St. John's until it was closed in 1955.

St. Francis Xavier church on St. George's Island

St. James parish, near St. Mary's City, was begun in 1915 as a mission of St. Michael's in Ridge. This parish, along with St. Peter Claver, was served in the first part of the century by two Jesuits, Father John LaFarge and then Father Horace McKenna, who were renowned in the county and beyond for their efforts on behalf of racial justice.

Holy Face in Great Mills

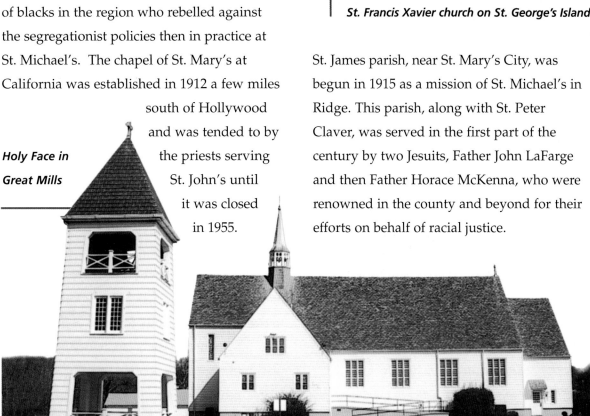

St. Peter Claver in St. Inigoes was established for African Americans in 1903.

Fr. Horace McKenna, S.J. (1899-1982) served the people of St. Peter Claver parish in St. Mary's County from 1931-1953. While there, he was a tireless promoter of Catholic educational opportunities for Blacks and for racial justice in the Church. In 1953 he was assigned to St. Aloysius parish in Washington and from there continued his zealous work for the poor.

The fourth parish established in St. Mary's during this period was Our Lady of the Wayside in Chaptico. At the time of its establishment Chaptico also became the Jesuit residence and base of operations in the western part of the county.

Although St. Mary's was comparatively rich in Catholic churches, Catholic schools did not take hold in the county until the end of the nineteenth century. Various efforts at establishing Catholic schools had been made over the years. However, the individual lay men and women who ran these one room schools, and the pastors who sponsored them, lacked the support necessary to make these establishments permanent. Perhaps the most notable of these efforts was the parochial school associated with Holy Face parish in Great Mills in the 1880's. The first Catholic school in the county to endure, St. Mary's Academy in Leonardtown, came about through the providential convergence of lay generosity, pastoral leadership and religious zeal. In 1884 Mrs. Mary Miles, a convert and former teacher, donated the recently purchased Rose Hill Farm to Father Charles Jenkins, S.J., pastor at St. Aloysius, with the provision that he give the property to any religious order willing to establish a Catholic school on the site. After 11 unsuccessful attempts to enlist an order of religious women to run the school, Father Jenkins' perseverance paid off when the Sisters of Charity of Nazareth, Kentucky accepted the challenge in 1885, opening St. Mary's Academy. As the co-foundress of the Sisters of Charity of Nazareth was Charles County native, Mother Catherine Spalding, it was fitting that her congregation would take the lead in establishing Catholics schools in Southern Maryland. Devoted to addressing the educational needs of the Catholic community, the Sisters of Charity were remarkably flexible in their administration of the Academy. At various times in its 96-year history the school operated on both the elementary and secondary levels, admitted boys as well as girls, and maintained a residence for boarders.

In 1908 the Jesuit Fathers purchased property not far from St. Mary's Academy for the purpose of establishing a secondary school for boys in the county. Unable to staff such an institution themselves the Jesuits succeeded in recruiting the Xaverian Brothers to open the new school, called Leonard Hall, in 1909. Changing educational needs in the county led the Xaverian Brothers to open Ryken High School in Leonardtown in 1956. These three institutions, St. Mary's Academy, Leonard Hall and Ryken High School, provided Catholic secondary education to St. Mary's County for over a century. The Xaverian Brothers gave up the administration of Leonard Hall in 1972. In 1982, a lack of teaching sisters and brothers, and reduced enrollment led St. Mary's Academy and Ryken High School to merge.

St. Mary's Academy in Leonardtown opened in 1885 under the auspices of the Sisters of Charity of Nazareth. It provided Catholic education for the local community for close to a century.

Mrs. Mary Miles, a convert and former school teacher, donated land in 1884 for the establishment of St. Mary's Academy in Leonardtown under the direction of the Sisters of Charity of Nazareth, Kentucky.

While the coming of the Sisters of Charity of Nazareth and the Xaverian Brothers to Leonardtown greatly advanced the opportunities for Catholic education in the central part of St. Mary's County, other communities continued to rely on the public schools. Notable efforts were made by the Jesuits and laity at Ridge to establish schools at the southern end of the county. A two-story wooden school was erected at St. Michael's in 1911. Beginning in 1916 under the administration of Father LaFarge, classes were offered at the church of St. James in Dameron. In 1918, Mrs. David McCarthy of Washington donated funds for the establishment of a free-standing school, St. David's, at St. James parish. A school for the black children of the parish, called St. Alphonsus, operated from 1916 until 1922. Concurrent with the opening of St. Alphonsus, St. Peter Claver School was opened in a two-room building for the children of that parish. Initially, all four of these small schools were conducted by lay women.

"The battles of the future..."

Archbishop Michael J. Curley (1879-1947), first Archbishop of Washington. The Irish-born Curley came to America to serve as a missionary in Florida where he defended the Church's right to operate schools for Blacks. Named Archbishop of Baltimore in 1921 and the first Archbishop of Washington in 1939, Curley was an aggressive champion of Catholic schools and a generous friend of the poor.

CATHOLIC EDUCATION IN ST. MARY'S COUNTY, as well as the rest of the Archdiocese, was energized by the advent of Michael J. Curley as the tenth Archbishop of Baltimore in November 1921. Born in Ireland in 1879, Curley entered the seminary in Rome in 1900 to be a missionary in the then sparsely settled state of Florida. After his 1904 ordination Father Curley was assigned as the pastor of a parish which encompassed 7,200 square miles. In 1914 he was consecrated Bishop of St. Augustine. He attracted national attention three years later when he battled a Florida state law which prevented the Catholic Church from educating black children. On the day of his installation in Baltimore Archbishop Curley made it clear that the establishment of Catholic schools, even before churches, would be his priority, stating emphatically: "The battles of the future will be fought on the fields of education." A year after his arrival, Curley created a diocesan schools office and over the next ten years the Archdiocese spent $10 million on school construction. The Catholics of St. Mary's County were among the first to benefit from Archbishop Curley's commitment to Catholic education. In 1922, the Sisters of St. Joseph of Hartford, Connecticut came to Ridge to take over the operation of St. Michael's and St. David's, consolidating the two schools ten years later. The Sisters of St. Joseph would go on to operate other schools in the county, notably

Holy Angels, Avenue

Church of the Little Flower, Bethesda

St. Francis de Sales, Rockpoint

St. Margaret of Scotland, Seat Pleasant

Shrine of the Most Blessed Sacrament, Washington, D.C.

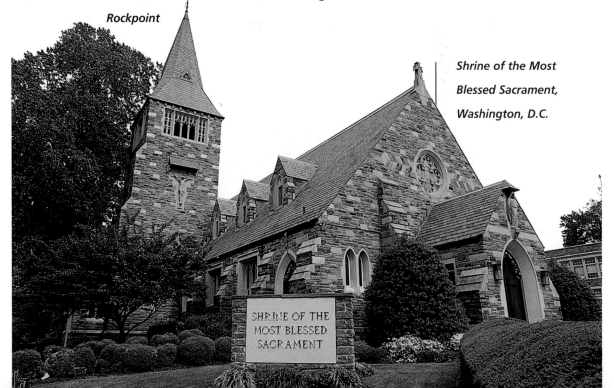

Holy Redeemer, College Park

St. Catherine of Alexandria, McConchie

Our Lady of Victory, Washington, D.C.

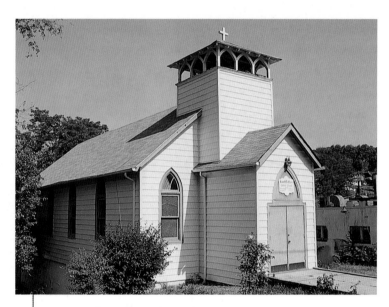

St. Matthias, Capitol Heights

Our Lady of Perpetual Help, Washington, D.C.

Assumption, Washington, D.C.

Mount Calvary, Forestville

St. Thomas, Apostle, Washington, D.C.

St. Gabriel, Washington, D.C.

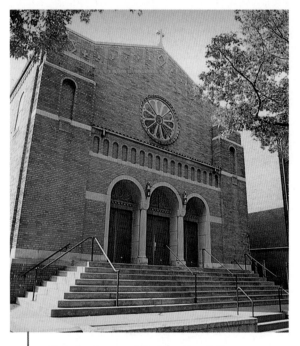

Holy Redeemer, Washington, D.C.

St. Martin of Tours, Gaithersburg

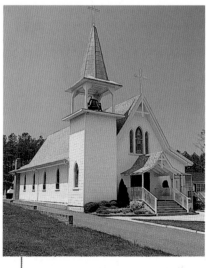

St. Mary, Star of the Sea, Indian Head

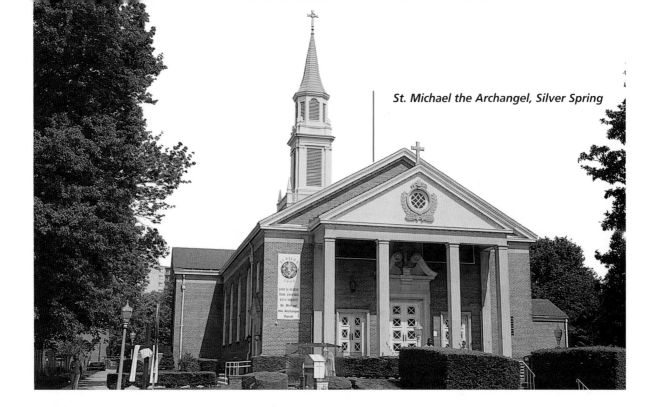

St. Michael the Archangel, Silver Spring

Epiphany, Washington, D.C.

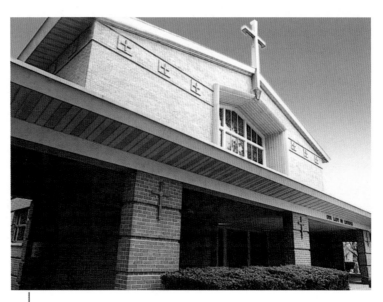

Our Lady of Lourdes, Bethesda

St. Michael, Baden

St. Mary, Landover Hills

Catholic Church of the Incarnation, Washington, D.C.

St. John Vianney, Prince Frederick

Our Lady of the Wayside, Chaptico

PART 4

"The Measure of Our Success," 1940-1979

> *"Permit me beloved priests and people, to place before you this thought—the measure of the success of God's Church in this new Archdiocese is not the splendid temples you have raised, not the schools you have built, not the institutions of charity, that stand all around us, but the measure of our success is the growth of the love of God in the soul of every man, woman and child..."*

"Aeque Principaliter"

ON MARCH 25, 1940, the Solemnity of the Annunciation and 306 years to the day from the first Mass on St. Clement's Island, another first Mass was held. This was the first Mass in the Cathedral of St. Matthew the Apostle in Washington, Archepiscopal Church of the newly erected Archdiocese of Washington. It was an event which undoubtedly elicited mixed emotions from its participants. For some, especially the Catholic inhabitants of the City of Washington, who at that time comprised the entire population of the new Archdiocese, the occasion granted the capital city of the United States the long overdue recognition which it deserved. Right from the start, even as the fields were being parceled out to form lots for the new city, there were those Catholics who envisioned

The interior of the Cathedral of St. Matthew

the day when Washington would be a cathedral city. To prepare for this eventuality, Archbishop Carroll's cousin, Daniel Carroll of Duddington, had presented him a lot in Washington for the building of a cathedral. Although "cathedral square" as it was called remained vacant until 1900, when it became the site of St. Vincent de Paul church, the notion that the nation's capital should have its own bishop continued to gain adherents until July 22, 1939, when, it was confirmed by Pope Pius XII in the apostolic constitution *Supremae Ecclesiasticae Postestatis.*

For others present for the first Mass at the "new" Cathedral of St. Matthew, including the first Archbishop of Washington, Michael J. Curley, it was a melancholy affair. For the Archdiocese of Baltimore, which already had been partitioned several times, having the Holy Father officially "disjoin" the city of Washington from her was seen as diminishing her importance. Previous Archbishops of Baltimore had resisted such a separation for this reason. Indeed, in Spring 1914, Cardinal Gibbons felt compelled to travel to Rome to prevent the establishment of Washington as a separate diocese. He proposed a compromise that the nation's capital be honored by having its name added to that of the premier see. Although Cardinal Gibbons' plea on behalf of Baltimore was successful even without his compromise, the same proposal would not be enough when made by Archbishop Curley in 1939. The war that had passed and the one just beginning had elevated the stature of the United States in the world to the level where

its national capital "should be adorned with the honor of an archepiscopal throne." Thus, Pius XII declared, while the new Archdiocese would be united to the metropolitan Church of Baltimore, under the common title, "Archdiocese of Baltimore-Washington," with the same bishop, and the same curia, the newest American see was *aeque principaliter,* "on the same level," with the oldest one.

Archbishop Curley's lack of enthusiasm for the elevation of Washington as an episcopal see separate from Baltimore was manifest in his reluctance to take possession of his new see. In fact, the Apostolic Delegate, Archbishop Amleto Cicognani, wrote to Curley in February 1940 warning that if he did not act on or before March 25, 1940, the title would expire. However, Curley did have the consolation of knowing that the two sees would remain together under his leadership for the duration of his tenure. This was in spite of President Roosevelt's efforts to have the new archdiocese placed under a bishop less critical of his administration's policies than Curley, particularly in regard to American involvement in the war in Europe and aid to the Soviets. Curley would continue his support for American neutrality until Pearl Harbor and his opposition to Communism until his death.

Still, while Archbishop Curley became the first Archbishop of Washington only reluctantly, he did not miss the opportunity of his installation to remind his listeners and

The Cathedral of St. Matthew

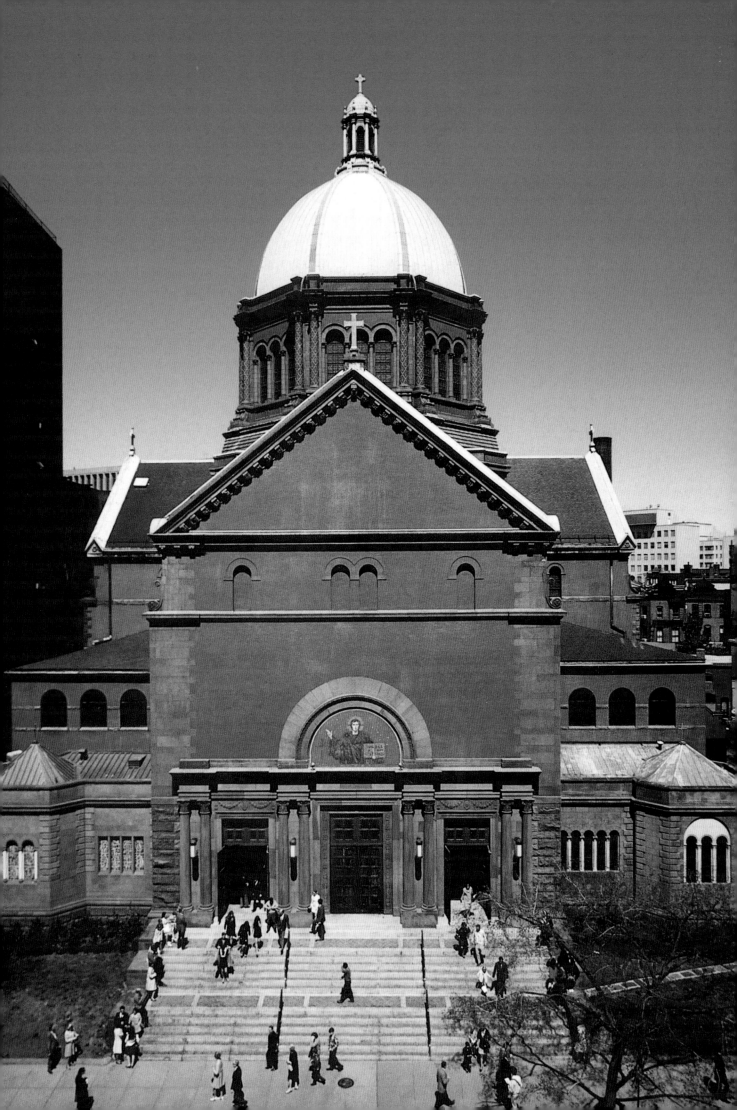

Archbishop Curley celebrates the establishment of the Archdiocese of Washington with a charity dinner at the Little Sisters of the Poor on March 25, 1940.

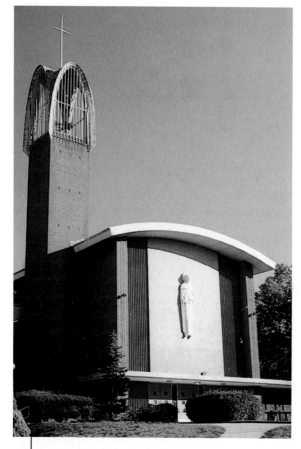

St. Bernard of Clairvaux, Riverdale

those who were to follow, that "the measure of our success" for the new Archdiocese "is the growth of the love of God" among all its inhabitants. Following the Mass, Archbishop Curley celebrated his installation by sponsoring a dinner for the elderly residing at the Little Sisters of the Poor in Washington.

Archbishop Curley's seven year tenure as Archbishop of Washington was largely consumed by the new challenges posed by the Second World War and its immediate aftermath. The city itself was bulging at the seams with new residents, having increased in population by 36.2 percent in the New Deal years, reaching 663,091 people in 1940. As a war capital, Washington's population would grow by a further 21 percent. War time rationing restricted new construction and hindered the growth of the suburbs. Despite this, six new parishes originated during these years. St. Bernard of Clairveaux (1942) in Riverdale and St. Bernadette (1944) in Silver Spring were opened in the growing suburbs of Prince George's and Montgomery Counties respectively. Two new parishes were started in the District itself, Our Lady Queen of Peace (1943) in Southeast

St. Bernadette, Silver Spring